We Come From

South Africa

ALISON BROWNLIE

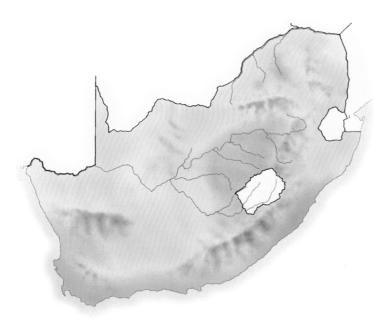

RSVP
RAINTREE
STECK-VAUGHN
PUBLISHERS
A Steck-Vaughn Company

Austin, Texas
www.steck-vaughn.com

WE COME FROM

Brazil • China • France
Germany • India • Jamaica • Japan
Kenya • Nigeria • South Africa

Many of the people you are about to meet live in a township in South Africa called Soweto. Like any other country, South Africa has many different lifestyles. People live in the country as well as in towns and cities.

Cover: Tshepo and his friends have a bicycle that they share.
Title page (from top to bottom): The rugged coast of the Western Cape; traditional tribal food preparation in a village; a wild white rhino in a game park; downtown Johannesburg; one of South Africa's many gold mines
Contents page: Children playing cricket together
Index: On weekends, Tshepo meets his friends at the playground.

© Copyright 2000, text, Steck-Vaughn Company

Published by Raintree Steck-Vaughn Publishers, an imprint of Steck-Vaughn Company

Acknowledgments: All the photographs in this book were taken by Gordon Clements, but thanks go also to Thomas Chauke, photographer with the Office of the Premier, Gauteng Province, for his invaluable assistance.

The map artwork on page 5 was produced by Peter Bull.

Library of Congress Cataloging-in-Publication Data
Brownlie, Alison.
South Africa / Alison Brownlie.
    p.   cm.—(We come from)
Includes bibliographical references and index.
Summary: Introduces the land, climate, industries, home life, schools, and leisure activities of South Africa.
ISBN 0-8172-5221-5
1. South Africa—Juvenile literature.
[1. South Africa.]
I. Title. II. Series.
DT1719.B76 2000
968—dc21   99-14211

Printed in Italy. Bound in the United States.
1 2 3 4 5 6 7 8 9 0 04 03 02 01 00

Contents

Welcome to South Africa!

"My name is Tshepo. Here I am with my mother and father and my big sister, Mathapelo, who is eleven."

Tshepo Mohasoane is seven years old. He lives with his parents and older sister in Soweto, a township near Johannesburg. Johannesburg is one of the largest cities in South Africa. Johannesburg is shown on the map on page 5.

▲ *From left to right: Mathapelo, Tshepo's father, Tshepo, and Tshepo's mother.*

▲ *South Africa's place in the world*

▼ *This book takes you to Soweto, as well as to the rest of South Africa.*

Pronunciation guide

	you say:
Tshepo	Sheppo
Mathapelo	Matta-pello
Mohasoane	Mohar-so-wahnay
Soweto	Swetto
Afrikaans	Afri-kahns
Sotho	Sotto

SOUTH AFRICA

Capital cities	Cape Town, Pretoria, and Bloemfontein
Land area	470,000 sq. mi. (1.2 million sq. km)
Population	44 million people
Main languages	English and Afrikaans and nine tribal languages, including Zulu, Xhosa, Tswana, and Sotho
Main religion	Christianity

5

The Land and Weather

South Africa is a big country. More than half the people live in large cities. Many people leave the country looking for work in the cities.

▶ *Playing jumbo chess in a city park in Johannesburg*

▼ *The flat veld farmland is good for growing wheat.*

The Drakensberg Mountains in the east of South Africa are the highest and wettest parts of the country. In the center there is a large area of land called the veld. This is a high, fairly flat plateau. Farther west again the land is lower and drier. In places it is almost a desert.

▲ *Its flat top has given this mountain the name of "Table Mountain." It is a famous tourist attraction near Cape Town.*

◄ *Many wild animals live in South Africa's game parks. As well as lions like this, there are elephants, zebra, leopards, monkeys, hippopotamuses, and many others.*

Look at the map on page 5 and you will see that South Africa has a long coastline. It has many beautiful beaches.

The summers are usually hot, and the winters are mild. Snow is unusual in South Africa, even on the high mountaintops.

▼ *One of South Africa's beautiful sandy beaches*

"In the summer, when it is hot and dry, I help my father water the garden."—Tshepo

9

At Home

A few years ago South Africa had strict laws to keep black and white people apart. They could not even use the same public toilet. This was known as Apartheid.

As a result of Apartheid, there are huge differences between the lives of whites and blacks. The white people are usually richer.

▲ *Tshepo likes to jump rope in his backyard.*

◀ *In many parts of Soweto people build their homes from recycled materials.*

▶ *These luxury houses are in Johannesburg.*

However, Tshepo's family is well off. They live in a one-story house with a small yard. Their house has a kitchen, a living room, a bathroom, and three bedrooms. They have a color TV, a stereo, and a microwave oven.

▲ *Children playing outside apartment buildings in Cape Town*

"I've got lots of colored pencils, and I like drawing and coloring."—Tshepo

◀ *Some houses do not have running water, so families collect it in metal drums or plastic containers.*

In the country people live on farms or in small villages. They collect water from a well, and only a very few have electricity. In the cities the larger houses have swimming pools, and wealthier families employ maids to do the housework.

▼ *In villages, many tasks are done outside, in the shade of a tree.*

Food and Cooking

Most people who live in the country villages grow vegetables for themselves. They grow potatoes, onions, and different kinds of cabbages. The food is often prepared and cooked outdoors.

In the country there are large modern farms that raise cattle, sheep, and goats. Most people like to eat meat, and barbecues are very popular. Sometimes the meat is cut into strips and dried. This meat is called *biltong*.

▲ *Barbecues are called* braai *in South Africa.*

▶ *On small farms people do most of the work by hand.*

"Hot cereal is my favorite food."—Tshepo

15

16

◄ *There are many different vegetables for sale in a city market.*

Wheat and corn grow well on the veld. People like to eat a type of cereal, or porridge, made from corn.

South Africa has a good climate for growing fruit such as oranges and apples. These are often sold to other countries. In the cities people enjoy eating in restaurants.

▶ *In Tshepo's house his mother does most of the cooking.*

◄ *Sifting the corn-meal, or "mealie," to make porridge*

At Work

Many people in the country work as farmers, growing the food they need. Some move to the cities to find work in offices and on building sites.

▼ *Some people work in the game parks, tending the wild animals.*

▲ *Many women in cities work in factories, making clothes.*

18

South Africa produces more gold and diamonds than any other country, and there are many jobs as miners.

Both Tshepo's parents work for the government. His mother works as a secretary.

"I work in a chemistry laboratory. I check that factories are not causing pollution."—Tshepo's dad

At School

Under the Apartheid laws, black and white children had to go to separate schools. But now schools are mixed.

Tshepo goes to Itemogele Primary School. There are 45 children in his class.

School starts at 8 o'clock and finishes at 2 o'clock in the afternoon. There are no school lunches, so Tshepo's mother makes him sandwiches.

▲ Tshepo and his friends run to make sure they are not late for school.

▼ Children working together around a computer in a city school

Tshepo learns math, handwriting, technology, art, science, and history. He also learns three languages, English, Afrikaans, and Sotho, which is his tribal language.

▼ *Children who go to school in the country learn about farming.*

Some parents at Tshepo's school pay for their children to have extra lessons. They want their children to have a good education.

▶ *All schoolchildren wear uniforms, although some parents find it difficult to afford them.*

"I have a lot of homework. Sometimes my mother helps me."—Tshepo

23

Spare Time

Many South Africans love to spend time outdoors, having barbecues and parties or playing sports. Rugby, cricket, and soccer are very popular. The South African soccer team reached the finals of the World Cup in 1998.

In the cities people enjoy going to the movies and theater.

▲ *A girl fishes from the pier in Cape Town.*

▶ *City children enjoying a game of street hockey*

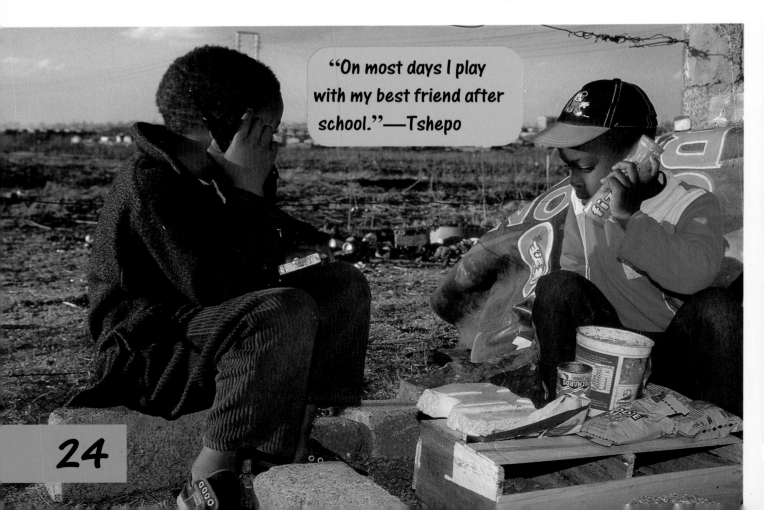

"On most days I play with my best friend after school."—Tshepo

Looking Ahead

Since 1994, all people in South Africa have been able to vote for whom they want to lead them. People are excited about the future and hope that there will be more opportunities for blacks as well as for whites.

▼ *More tourists visit South Africa now that Apartheid is over.*

"When I am older, I want to be a policeman so that I can arrest criminals."—Tshepo

27

How to Play Hopscotch

Tshepo and his friends enjoy playing hopscotch. They draw a hopscotch plan on the ground with chalk and number the squares from 1 to 10.

- First, throw a stone into square 1.

- Hop over square 1 into square 2.

- Hop into squares 3 and 4, landing with one foot in each.

- Then hop into square 5, jump into squares 6 and 7, hop into square 8, and jump into squares 9 and 10.

- Then jump completely around and land in squares 9 and 10, facing the way you have come.

- Hop and jump back again in the same way, stopping on square 2.

- Standing on one leg, pick up the stone from square 1 and hop over it.

- Start again, this time throwing the stone into square 2, then square 3 and so on.

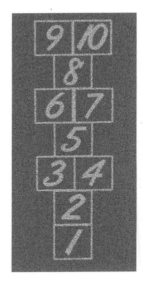

▲ *There are different ways to draw hopscotch plans. This is one of them.*

- You miss a turn if

(a) your stone does not land in the right square

(b) you accidentally step into the same square as the stone.

The winner is the first person to pick up the stone from square 10 and get back to the start.

◄ *Tshepo must not step in the square with the stone. He hops over it.*

South Africa Fact File

◀ Money Facts

South African money is the Rand. There are 100 cents in one Rand.

Independence Day

South Africa has a national holiday on May 31, which is Independence Day. This is the day when all South Africans were able to vote for the first time.

◀ Flag and Anthem

After Apartheid, South Africa had a new flag and new national anthem, "God Bless Africa." The six colors of the flag include the colors of all the political parties in South Africa.

River Facts

The longest river in South Africa is the Orange River. It is 1,300 mi. (2,090 km) long.

Nelson Mandela

The most famous South African is Nelson Mandela. He spent 27 years in prison before becoming South Africa's first democratically elected president in 1994.

▶ National Park

Kruger National Park is the largest game park in South Africa. It is about 7,700 sq. mi. (20,000 sq. km). It was founded in 1926 and contains hundreds of different kinds of animals.

World's Largest Diamond

The largest diamond in the world was found in South Africa in 1905. It weighed 1.37 lbs. (0.62 kg). It was cut into 105 smaller gems. To find 3 tons of diamonds, 30 million tons of earth have to be dug out of the ground.

▼ Stamps

Many South African stamps show pictures of their wonderful wild animals.

Glossary

Afrikaans The language spoken by Afrikaners, the descendants of Dutch settlers.

Apartheid The system that kept black and white people apart.

Democracy A government freely elected by all the adult people.

Desert A place where it hardly ever rains and very few plants can grow.

Game Parks Special areas of land where wild animals are protected.

Plateau A very large and often flat-topped area of land.

Recycled materials Materials that are used again and again to make different things.

Townships These were separate areas on the edges of large cities where black people had to live during Apartheid.

Tribal languages The languages spoken by different groups of African people.

Further Information

Books to Read

Blauer, Ettagale. *South Africa* (Enchantment of the World). Danbury, CT: Children's Press, 1998.

Canesso, Claudia. *South Africa* (Major World Nations). New York: Chelsea House, 1998.

Green, Jen. *A Family from South Africa* (Families Around the World). Austin, TX: Raintree Steck-Vaughn, 1998.

Rosmarin, Ike. *South Africa* (Cultures of the World). Tarrytown, NY: Benchmark Books, 1996.

Ryan, Pat. *South Africa* (Faces and Places). Plymouth, MN: Child's World, 1997.

Useful Addresses:
South African Embassy
3051 Massachusetts Avenue
Washington, DC 20008

South African Tourism Board
747 Third Avenue
New York, NY 10017

Index

All the numbers in **bold** refer to photographs.